# Learn to Think

Basic exercises in the core thinking
skills for ages 6–11

## John Langrehr

Routledge
Taylor & Francis Group

LONDON AND NEW YORK

First published by Curriculum Corporation in Australia in 2003
Reprinted 2003

Published 2008
by Routledge
2 Park Square, Milton Park, Abingdon, Oxon OX14 4RN

Simultaneously published in the USA and Canada
by Routledge
270 Madison Avenue, New York, NY 10016

*Routledge is an imprint of the Taylor & Francis Group, an informa
business*

© 2008 John Langrehr

Each publisher will be responsible for the registration and any
necessary defence of copyright in its own territory.

Printed and bound in Great Britain by Bell & Bain, Ltd., Glasgow

*British Library Cataloguing in Publication Data*
A catalogue record for this book is available from the British Library

*Library of Congress Cataloging-in-Publication Data*
Langrehr, John.
  Learn to think : basic exercises in the core thinking skills for ages
  6-11 / John Langrehr.
      p. cm. – (Thinking lessons)
  ISBN 978–0–415–46590–8
  1. Thought and thinking – Study and teaching. 2. Elementary
  school teaching. I. Title.
  LB1590.3.L37 2008
  370.15'2–dc22
  2007048651

ISBN 10: 0-415-46590-7 (pbk)
ISBN 10: 0-203-92645-5 (ebk)
ISBN 13: 978-0-415-46590-8 (pbk)
ISBN 13: 978-0-203-92645-1 (ebk)

# Contents

# Introduction

Pupils need to be taught content to think about. They also need to be taught **thinking processes** which they can use to think about this content. In other words, they need to learn some good questions to ask themselves when thinking about content in different ways. 'Metacognition' (thinking about thinking) empowers them, giving them a wide repertoire of useable cognitive tools. Curriculum planners assume that students learn these processes quite naturally, but research shows that this is not so.

We regularly use about twenty basic or **core thinking processes** to connect and make sense of information. These are listed on the contents page. The exercises in this book allow pupils to practise these processes and to learn the questions that are useful to ask themselves when they use them.

The thinking processes in the book are related to **organisational**, **analytical**, **critical** or **evaluative** and **creative thinking**. The content covered involves mathematics, language, social studies, and science.

Each lesson in the book starts with **introductory notes** (the first page of the lesson) for teachers to discuss with pupils. This page also includes an **example** for the teacher to work through as an explanation about what is wanted in the exercise which will follow. When the thinking process is understood, pupils can work through the items on their photocopied **student worksheets.**

Some **suggested answers** are then provided. And finally, some **useful questions** for pupils to ask themselves when thinking in the different ways is provided at the end of most exercises. Teachers can share these with pupils to note down at the end of their own worksheets. The lists of processing questions can be thought of as mental thinking programs for comparing, categorising, distinguishing facts from opinions, generalising, and so on.

This book provides enough exercises for it to be used as the **basis of a thinking skills programme** for pupils in about the ages of 6–11.

John Langrehr

# Observing Properties

- Everything about us made by human beings or by nature has a design.
- The design or composition of any given thing is special and is that way for a particular reason. Bottles don't just happen to be made of glass rather than other materials. Stop lights don't just happen to be red rather than other colours. And trees don't just happen to have thousands of leaves rather than 10 or 20.
- We say that the design of a given thing fits a particular purpose.
- We all see things but we usually don't ask ourselves **why** something has the design that it does, rather than some other design.

- Lesson 1 gets you looking at things more carefully or thoughtfully.
- If you look at, and think about, the world about you, life will become so much more interesting. You will begin to understand why creators designed things the way they did.

- To help you focus on the properties of something you are observing remember the acronym **SCUMPS**. Each letter of this word helps you to ask yourself why something has the **S**ize, **C**olour, **U**se, **M**aterial, **P**arts, and **S**hape that it does, rather than other possibilities.

### Example

| Object | Properties | Reasons for properties |
|---|---|---|
| brick | rough<br>heavy<br>geometric shape | cement sticks to its surface easily<br>wind won't blow it away<br>easy to stack on each other in rows |

Write in three properties that you have noticed for each of the following things. After each property write in a reason why you think the thing has this property.

| Object | Properties | Reasons for properties |
|---|---|---|
| coin | •<br>•<br>• | •<br>•<br>• |
| flag | •<br>•<br>• | •<br>•<br>• |
| tree | •<br>•<br>• | •<br>•<br>• |
| car tyre | •<br>•<br>• | •<br>•<br>• |
| a bottle | •<br>•<br>• | •<br>•<br>• |
| a football | •<br>•<br>• | •<br>•<br>• |

## Useful questions to ask myself when OBSERVING

- 
-

# Lesson One

| Object | Properties | Reasons for properties |
|---|---|---|
| coin | round<br>metallic<br>thin<br>face | easy to handle/store<br>won't bend easily<br>light<br>country's history |
| flag | coloured<br>patterned<br>made of cloth<br>rectangular | easy to see<br>represents people<br>difficult to tear<br>easy to make |
| tree | leaves<br>roots<br>round trunk<br>upright | take in gases<br>keep tree stable<br>provide strength<br>to reach for sunlight |
| car tyre | round<br>rubber<br>hollow<br>grooved | smooth to roll<br>flexible<br>for flexing<br>grip on road |
| a bottle | made of glass<br>round sides<br>narrow neck<br>flat bottom | easy to clean/see through<br>for strength<br>easy to pour<br>easy to stand up |
| a football | made of leather<br>oval shape<br>hollow | easy to catch/kick<br>easy to catch/kick, random bounce<br>light, easy to kick |

## Useful questions to ask when OBSERVING

- What size, colour, use, material, parts, and shape (SCUMPS) does this thing have?

- Why does this thing have this size, colour, use, material, parts, and shape rather than other sizes, colours, uses, materials, parts, and shapes?

# Observing Similarities

- I wonder if you have thought about how two or more things are **similar**?

- For example, you have seen lemons and bananas but have you ever asked yourself what is **alike** about these two fruits?

- Can we come up with at least four ways in which these fruits are similar?

- Remember the word **SCUMPS** from Lesson 1? Are the
  **S**ize,
  **C**olour,
  **U**se,
  **M**aterial,
  **P**arts, or
  **S**hape of these fruits similar?

| Example | |
|---|---|
| **Things** | **similar properties** |
| banana lemon  | both: • yellow<br>• food<br>• thick skins<br>• grow on trees |

# Lesson Two

| Things | 3 similar properties |
|---|---|
| flowers<br>birds | •<br>•<br>• |
| road<br>river | •<br>•<br>• |
| chair<br>horse | •<br>•<br>• |
| door<br>book | •<br>•<br>• |
| the numbers<br>4 and 9 | •<br>•<br>• |
| the words<br>fell, ran | •<br>•<br>• |
| a square<br>a circle | •<br>•<br>• |

## Questions to ask myself when OBSERVING SIMILARITIES

- 
-

## Possible answers

| Things | 3 similar properties |
|---|---|
| flowers<br>birds | living, need sun/air/water, different types/colours |
| road<br>river | have names, carry transport, have start and end |
| chair<br>horse | can sit on, four legs, different heights, different colours |
| door<br>book | made of wood/tree, rectangular, human made, can open |
| the numbers<br>4 and 9 | both single digits, have exact square root, divide into 36 |
| the words<br>fell, ran | both verbs, have one vowel, are past tense<br>have no capitals, pattern of consonant/vowel/consonant |
| a square<br>a circle | closed figures, 2D, geometric shapes |

## Useful questions to ask yourself when OBSERVING SIMILARITIES

• What size, colour, use, material, parts, and shape (SCUMPS) do these things have?

• Do these things both have the *same* size, colour, use, material, parts, and shape?

# Observing Differences

It is also useful to notice how things are **different** from each other. For example, a cat and a dog may be similar in that they are both living, both animals, both have four legs, or both eat meat. However, only a cat can meow or climb trees. A useful fact next time you are chased by a wild dog! This lesson checks if you have noticed and stored small **differences** between things.

## Example

| Things | 3 Different Properties |
|---|---|
| *cat*<br>dog | *only a cat can*: • climb trees<br>• meow<br>• chase mice |

Learn to Think

| Things | 3 Different properties |
|---|---|
| *chair*<br>table | *chair only*<br>•<br>•<br>• |
| *crab*<br>fish | *crab only*<br>•<br>•<br>• |
| *circle*<br>triangle | *circle only*<br>•<br>•<br>• |
| *number 4*<br>number 11 | *number 4 only*<br>•<br>•<br>• |
| *newspaper*<br>book | *newspaper only*<br>•<br>•<br>• |
| *artery*<br>vein | *artery only*<br>•<br>•<br>• |
| *president*<br>queen | *president only*<br>•<br>•<br>• |
| *democracy*<br>dictatorship | *democracy only*<br>•<br>•<br>• |
| *pencil*<br>nail | *pencil only*<br>•<br>• |
| *bird*<br>bee | *bird only*<br>•<br>•<br>• |

## Questions to ask myself when OBSERVING DIFFERENCES

•

# Lesson Three

| Things | 3 Different properties |
|---|---|
| *chair* and table | *chair* meant for sitting on, one per person, can be padded |
| *crab* and fish | *crab* has claws, a hard shell, swims backwards, can live out of water |
| *circle* and triangle | *circle* has no straight sides or angles or vertices |
| *numbers* 4 and 11 | *4* is even, not a prime number, only one digit |
| *newspaper* and book | *newspaper* is low cost, daily, many writers, current news |
| *artery* and vein | *artery* has thick walls, carries blood from heart, fewer in number |
| *democracy* and dictatorship | leaders elected by people, freedom of speech, people free to travel from country |
| *president* and queen | head of government, elected, can be a man |
| *bird* and bee | bird has two legs, blood, bones, lives longer |

# Categorising

- We categorise or place **similar things** into **groups** or **categories** that we then store in our brains. These categories are like topic folders.
- In our 'mental filing cabinet' we have files labeled 'red things', 'living things', 'large wild animals', and so on.
- By organising things into categories it is easy for us to quickly come up with examples of a category when we have to.
- The greater the number of things we carefully observe and compare, the greater the number of examples in the categories stored in our brain.
- The items in this lesson will test the kinds of labels you have used to categorise things in your mental filing cabinet.

## Example

| Things | Same because they are all... |
|---|---|
| Venus<br>Earth<br>Saturn | planets |

# Lesson Four

The THREE things in the following groups are the SAME in some way. Write in one or more ways in which they are the same?

| Things | Same because they are all... |
|---|---|
| scissors, magnet, nail | |
| ant, beetle, butterfly | |
| ice, fog, steam | |
| coal, sunlight, uranium | |
| lever, ramp, pulley | |
| cotton, wool, hemp | |
| photograph, page, door | |
| tyre, coin, ball | |
| cork, iceberg, apple | |
| the numbers 7, 11, 13 | |
| triangles, squares, polygons | |
| the words walk, catch, climb | |
| plants, animal, insects | |

## Questions to ask myself when CATEGORISING

- 
- 

Learn to Think

## Possible answers

| Things | Same because they are all... |
|---|---|
| scissors, magnet, nail | made of metal or machine made |
| ant, beetle, butterfly | insects |
| ice, fog, steam | made of water |
| coal, sunlight, uranium | used to produce electricity |
| lever, ramp, pulley | machines to make work easier |
| cotton, wool, hemp | natural fibres |
| photograph, page door | rectangular, human made |
| tyre, coin, ball | round |
| cork, iceberg, apple | float on water |
| the numbers 7, 11, 13 | odd or prime numbers |
| triangles, squares, pentagons | polygons, geometric figures |
| the words *walk, catch, climb* | verbs |
| plants, animals, insects | living things |

# Questions to ask yourself when CATEGORISING

• Do these things have a similar size, colour, use, material, parts, shape, or some other property?

# Comparing

- We have looked at similarities (Lesson 2) and differences (Lesson 3). Can they be combined?
- Yes. It is possible to think about how two things are **different** and how they are the **same**.
- Again, it might help you to think about the size, colour, use, material, parts and shape (SCUMPS) of the two things you are comparing.

## Example

| Sharks only (differences) | Both sharks *and* cats (similarities) | Cats only (differences) |
|---|---|---|
| swim<br>no legs<br>have gills | eat meat<br>have blood<br>have tails | meow<br>climb trees<br>kept as pets |

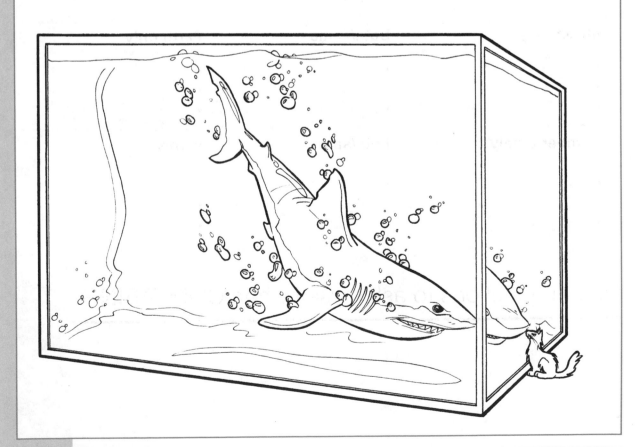

Learn to Think

| Possible answers | | |
|---|---|---|
| **trees only** | **both/same** | **insects only** |
| • <br> • <br> • | • <br> • <br> • | • <br> • <br> • |
| **dinosaurs only** | **both/same** | **elephants only** |
| • <br> • <br> • | • <br> • <br> • | • <br> • <br> • |
| **snails only** | **both/same** | **crabs only** |
| • <br> • <br> • | • <br> • <br> • | • <br> • <br> • |
| **chess only** | **both/same** | **football only** |
| • <br> • <br> • | • <br> • <br> • | • <br> • <br> • |
| **moon only** | **both/same** | **earth only** |
| • <br> • <br> • | • <br> • <br> • | • <br> • <br> • |
| **number 8 only** | **both/same** | **9 only** |
| • <br> • <br> • | • <br> • <br> • | • <br> • <br> • |

## Useful questions to ask myself when COMPARING

- 
-

# Lesson Five

| trees only | both/same | insects only |
|---|---|---|
| made of wood<br>roots<br>sap | made of cells<br>need water, air<br>can reproduce | head, eyes<br>move along<br>lay eggs, fly |
| **dinosaurs only** | **both/same** | **elephants only** |
| extinct<br>reptile<br>long neck | plant-eaters<br>big legs<br>big body | living<br>mammal<br>no eggs |
| **snails only** | **both/same** | **crabs only** |
| live on land<br>eat greens<br>have slime<br>out at night | shells<br>slow moving<br>living<br>reproduce | live in water and land<br>eat meat<br>can nip<br>claws |
| **chess only** | **both/same** | **football only** |
| pieces<br>individuals<br>board | players<br>rules<br>winner | teams<br>use ball<br>field |
| **moon only** | **both/same** | **earth only** |
| no life<br>no water<br>no air | round<br>move around sun<br>reflect sunlight | life<br>has water<br>has air |
| **number 8 only** | **both/same** | **9 only** |
| even number<br>divides evenly into 80<br>not a perfect square | less than 10<br>divides into 72<br>has factors | odd number<br>divides by 3<br>perfect square |

## Useful questions to ask yourself when COMPARING

- What is a property (SCUMPS) that the first thing has?

- Does the second thing have this property?

# Ordering in Terms of Size and Time

## Ordering by Size

- In our brains we can also organise things in an **order** or **sequence**. For example, we order things in terms of such things as their size, speed, cost, and so on.
- Ordering and comparing things is all part of connecting them together in our memories in an organised way.

| Example | |
|---|---|
| **Jumbled things** | **Order in decreasing size** |
| forest<br>branch<br>tree<br>twig | forest, tree, branch, twig |

# Lesson Six

## Student worksheet

The following related things are placed out of order. Rewrite them in order of their **size** starting with the **largest**.

| **Jumbled things** | **Order in decreasing size** |
|---|---|
| sentence, paragraph, word | |
| lane, path, highway, road | |
| speech, act, scene, play | |
| artery, blood system, body, heart | |
| planet, universe, moon, sun | |
| reflex angle, acute angle, obtuse angle, right angle | |
| retina, eye, sensory system, rod | |
| crystal, molecule, atom, nucleus | |
| asian, humanity, race, chinese | |
| nation, community, daughter, family | |
| catholic, priest, culture, religion | |

## Useful questions to ask myself when ORDERING IN TERMS OF SIZE

- 
-

## Possible answers

| Jumbled things (unordered) | Order in decreasing size |
|---|---|
| sentence, paragraph, word | paragraph, sentence, word |
| lane, path, highway, road | highway, road, lane, path |
| speech, act, scene, play | play, act, scene, speech |
| artery, blood system, body, heart | boy, blood system, heart, artery |
| planet, universe, moon sun | universe, sun, planet, moon |
| reflex angle, acute angle, obtuse angle, right angle | reflex, obtuse, right, acute |
| retina, eye, sensory system, rod | sensory system, eye, retina, rod |
| crystal, molecule, atom, nucleus | crystal, molecule, atom, nucleus |
| asian, humanity, race, chinese | humanity, race, asian, chinese |
| nation, community, daughter, family | nation, community, family, daughter |
| catholic, priest, culture, religion | culture, religion, catholic, priest |

## Useful questions to ask when ORDERING in terms of SIZE

- Which thing contains all of the other things? (the largest)

- Which thing is part of ALL of the other things? (the smallest)

- Which thing is second largest? (contains the other things except the largest)

# Lesson Six

## Ordering by Time

- As you have just seen, we order things in terms of their size, often without being told to do this.
- We also **order** things **in time,** or **when they happen** in a sequence.
- The example below serves as an illustration of **chronological** (time) **order**.

### Example

| Jumbled things | Order first to last occurring |
|---|---|
| cocoon, caterpillar, egg, butterfly | egg, caterpillar, cocoon, butterfly |

## Student worksheet

The following things are not in an order. Rewrite them in order of the **time** that they occur in the sequence they belong to. Start with the **first** thing in the sequence.

| Jumbled things | Order first to last occurring |
| --- | --- |
| dusk, midday, dawn, midnight | |
| thunder, flood, lightning, rain | |
| clock, sundial, sun, sand timer | |
| election, nomination, campaign | |
| compose, rehearse, perform | |
| mill, harvest, bake, eat | |
| landscape, design, paint, build | |
| car, space craft, plane, bicycle | |

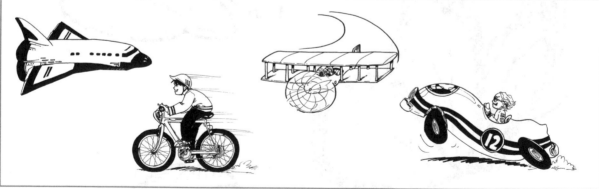

# Useful questions to ask myself when ORDERING IN TERMS OF TIME

- 
- 

Learn to Think

# Lesson Six

| Jumbled things | Order first to last occuring |
|---|---|
| dusk, midday, dawn, midnight | dawn, midday, dusk, midnight |
| thunder, flood, lightning, rain | lightning, thunder, rain, flood |
| clock, sundial, sun, sand timer | sun, sun dial, sand timer, clock |
| election, nomination, campaign | nomination, campaign, election |
| compose, rehearse, perform | compose, rehearse, perform |
| mill, harvest, bake, eat | harvest, mill, bake, eat |
| landscape, design, paint, build | design, build, paint, landscape |
| car, space craft, plane, bicycle | bicycle, car, plane, space craft |

## Useful questions to ask yourself when ORDERING IN TERMS OF TIME

- What has to happen first before the other things take place?

- What happens after all the other things have taken place?

# Thinking about Concepts

- Let's consider how we develop **ideas** or **concepts**. We'll start with a simple example.
- What are some of the properties, or distinctive things, about a fruit?
- Answers: skin, grows on trees, seeds, juice, sweet taste, coloured, we eat them.
- Is there any fruit that DOESN'T have any of these properties? Let's cross them off our list. Lemon is not sweet, pineapples/grapes don't grow on trees, some grapes don't have seeds.
- All of the properties left are **common to all** examples of fruit. We call this our **generalisation** or **concept** or mental picture of **all fruits**.
- If we had to describe a fruit to a man from Mars, this would be our generalisation or picture for him, as it is true for **all fruit**!
- Here is another example of a **concept**.

## Example

| Thing | Properties |
|-------|------------|
| a bird | nest, lays eggs, two legs, feathers, tail, chirps, head, no teeth |

# Lesson Seven

- Write down three or more properties of each thing.
- With your friends create a big list of facts for each thing.
- Then cross out the facts that are NOT TRUE for ALL examples of the thing you are considering.
- The properties left are called your CONCEPT, or generalisation of a thing.

| Thing | Properties |
|-------|-----------|
| a coin | |
| a stamp | |
| a car | |
| a square | |
| a poem | |
| a planet | |
| fruit | |
| a flower | |
| a game | |
| a culture | |
| trees | |

## Possible answers

| Thing | Properties |
| --- | --- |
| a coin | round, metallic, date, country, face on front, value |
| a stamp | rectangular, rough edge, date, country, price, sticky back |
| a car | wheels, motor, tyres, steering wheel, brake, fuel tank |
| a square | 4 straight and equal sides, 4 angles, an area, closed figure, diagonal |
| a poem | letters, sound, meaning, 'images', can be written |
| a planet | orbit, circles the sun, atmosphere, circular, found in space, reflects sunlight, turns on axis |
| fruit | skin, juice, coloured, we eat them |
| a flower | petals, colour, leaves, perfume, nectar stamens, attracts bees, pollen |
| a game | rules, players, winner, score, a finish, enjoyment |
| a culture | ways of a group of people, have special religions, food, dress, customs |
| trees | branches, roots, trunk, leaves, sap |

Organisational Thinking

Learn to Think

# Generalising

- In Lesson 7, we looked at how we make up a **generalisation** or general **concept** of something. Now let's develop this further.
- Think of all the **birds** you have seen in books or in real life.
- Do they have anything in common? It depends on how many you have seen. However, somewhere in your brain you have a picture of a bird with feathers, a beak, eggs, a nest, flying, and so on. This is your **generalisation** about or concept of a bird.
- Why do we generalise? Well, it is like a template or model to guide out thinking. It helps us to recognise new examples of birds. And it helps us to predict what a new bird that we observe might be able to do.
- As well as birds, you also have mental pictures of cars, chairs, triangles, and many other things. Following are examples using 'fruit' as the concept.

## Examples

| | Some Properties | | | |
|---|---|---|---|---|
| Fruit | coloured skin | grows on trees | sweet taste | seeds |
| apples | yes | yes | yes | yes |
| lemons | yes | yes | no | yes |
| strawberries | yes | no | yes | yes |
| bananas | yes | yes | yes | yes |
| passion fruit | yes | no | yes | yes |

Generalisation: fruit are generally coloured, and have skin and seeds.

## Useful questions to ask when GENERALISING

- Can I picture in my mind five or more examples of this thing?
- What are some parts or features of these examples?
- Can I list them?
- Which parts or features are COMMON to ALL EXAMPLES on my list?

Learn to Think

**1.** Write down four or more properties or features that are common to **all** examples of **coins** that you know of. These are generalizations about coins.

_____
_____
_____
_____

**2.** Write down four or more properties or features that are comon to **all** examples of **stamps** that you know of. These are generalizations about stamps.

_____
_____
_____
_____

**3.** Write down five to ten examples of **sports**. Now write down as many properties or features of these sports as you can. When you have done this, cross out any features that are **not** common to all the examples you gave.The features left are your generalizations about **all** sports.

_____
_____
_____

Properties      _____
                _____
                _____

Generalizations _____
                _____
                _____

# Lesson Eight

In questions 4 to 6 that follow, write in 'yes' if the examples given contain the property at the top of the columns. Write in 'no' if it doesn't have the property. Which properties do **all** of the examples given for a question have in common?

### 4.

| mammals | legs | swim | lungs | warm blood | fly | backbone |
|---|---|---|---|---|---|---|
| humans whales dogs bats | | | | | | |

Generalization:

### 5.

| metals | conduct electricity | solid | magnetic | melt easily |
|---|---|---|---|---|
| iron aluminum tin mercury | | | | |

Generalization:

### 6.

| insects | 6 legs | 3 body segments | antennae | wings | eyes |
|---|---|---|---|---|---|
| grass hopper beetle fly ant bee | | | | | |

Generalization:

Useful questions to ask myself when MAKING GENERALISATIONS

- 
-

1. All coins are generally made of metal, round, thin, hard, have a date.

2. All stamps generally have a country on front, made of paper, have rough edge, date, value on front.

3. All sports generally have players, sides, rules, winners, an umpire.

4. **Some Properties**

| mammals | legs | swim | lungs | warm blood | fly | backbone |
|---|---|---|---|---|---|---|
| humans | yes | yes | yes | yes | no | yes |
| whales | no | yes | yes | yes | no | yes |
| dogs | yes | yes | yes | yes | no | yes |
| bats | yes | no | yes | yes | yes | yes |

Generalization: All mammals have lungs, warm blood and a backbone.

5. **Some Properties**

| metals | conduct electricity | solid | magnetic | melt easily |
|---|---|---|---|---|
| iron | yes | yes | yes | no |
| aluminum | yes | yes | no | yes |
| tin | yes | yes | no | no |
| mercury | yes | no | no | yes |

Generalization: All metals conduct electricity.

6. **Some Properties**

| insects | 6 legs | 3 body segments | antennae | wings | eyes |
|---|---|---|---|---|---|
| grass hopper | yes | yes | yes | yes | yes |
| beetle | yes | yes | yes | yes | yes |
| fly | yes | yes | yes | yes | yes |
| ant | yes | yes | yes | some | yes |
| bee | yes | yes | yes | yes | yes |

Generalization: All insects have 6 legs, 3 body parts, antennae and eyes.

# Concept Maps

Having dealt with how we create concepts (Lessons 1-8), let's think about how we can organise them on paper. An important thinking tool is the 'picture summary' or **concept map**.

The KEY TERMS in any topic can be drawn! They are best summarised on a pictorial summary map which shows the relationships of different elements in the concept or process. Research shows that **visual mapping** increases both recall and understanding. Why? Because key terms and their connections become clear (separated from less relevant detail).

One good picture summary can save you writing hundreds of words. Concept maps simplify and clarify the main points of a concept or process and so help you to think clearly.

## Some standard concept map shapes include:

- **Overlapping circles:** 2 terms are being compared

- **Hierarchical:** a large term broken down into smaller and smaller parts

- **Fish bone:** several terms are causes leading to an effect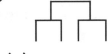

- **Radial:** several aspects of a central term are described

- **Flow chart:** stages of a linear process are discussed

- **Cyclical map:** stages of a cyclic process are discussed

- **Table:** 3 or more things are being compared

- **Interacting map:** interactions between people/things are described

How does it work? You have to identify the main terms or words and then write them in on a picture or map. Different shaped maps are available, so it is good to choose a map whose shape matches the shape of the ideas in your reading.

Look at the example of a picture summary map here.

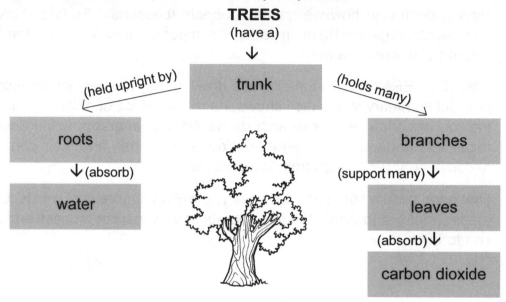

**TREES**
(have a)
↓

trunk

(held upright by) ←

(holds many) →

roots

branches

↓ (absorb)

(support many) ↓

water

leaves

(absorb) ↓

carbon dioxide

**1.** Fill in the missing words (?) on the maps below

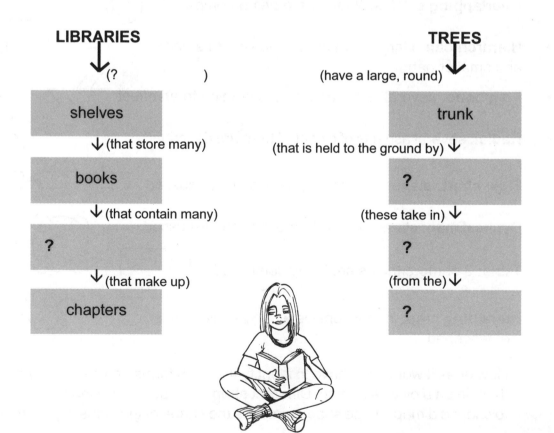

**LIBRARIES**
↓ (?                )

shelves

↓ (that store many)

books

↓ (that contain many)

?

↓ (that make up)

chapters

**TREES**
↓ (have a large, round)

trunk

(that is held to the ground by) ↓

?

(these take in) ↓

?

(from the) ↓

?

# Lesson Nine

**2.** Complete this summary map.

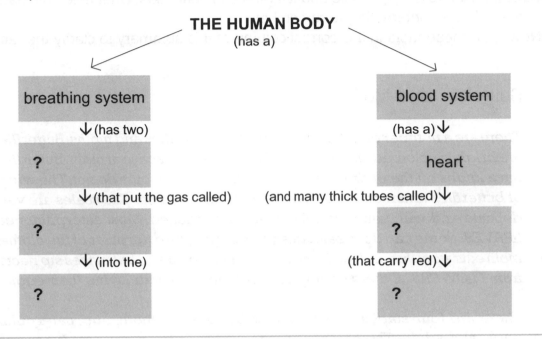

**THE HUMAN BODY**
(has a)

breathing system                 blood system

↓ (has two)                      (has a) ↓

?                                heart

↓ (that put the gas called)      (and many thick tubes called) ↓

?                                ?

↓ (into the)                     (that carry red) ↓

?                                ?

**3.** Try to make up a summary map for these terms:

**sides, quadrilaterals, diagonals, squares, rectangles, angles**

**4.** Look at the summary below for comparing TWO THINGS. It is used to summarise and clarify things that are different, and things that are the same, about two things.

| Cats only | Both | Dogs only |
|-----------|------|-----------|
|           |      |           |

**5.** Fill in the summary below with some features of bicycles and cars.

| Cars only | Both | Bicycles only |
|-----------|------|---------------|
|           |      |               |

**6a).** Read the following article about moths and butterflies. Underline any features of them that are interesting to remember.

Now write these facts in the correct column of this summary to clarify the facts.

## Butterflies and Moths

There are a number of differences between butterflies and moths. Butterflies are brightly coloured and fly by day. Most moths are active at night. Butterflies have knobs on the ends of their antenna, but most moths do not. The wings of butterflies and moths are covered with small scales. The scales are very delicate and will come off if the wings are touched. Most caterpillars eat LEAVES. Some can do great damage to crops. The caterpillar of the clothes moth eats wool, fur, and feathers. Some adult moths and butterflies sip nectar from FLOWERS. Others do not feed and die soon after laying their eggs.

There are four stages in the life of a butterfly or moth: egg, caterpillar, pupa, and adult. The caterpillar is the larva or young insect. It has soft, worm-like body. There are three pairs of true legs behind the head and several pairs of prolegs, or false legs, at the rear end.

After it has been eating for some time, the caterpillar forms a pupa. The pupa of a butterfly is called a chrysalis. It is a hard case in which the adult develops. When the adult has developed, it crawls out of the pupa. Most moth caterpillars spin a silk cocoon around themselves before turning into a pupa. Cocoons of the silk moth are used for making silk fabrics.

| Moths only | Both | Butterflies |
|------------|------|-------------|
|            |      |             |
|            |      |             |
|            |      |             |
|            |      |             |
|            |      |             |

**6b)**. Look at the picture summary map here for summarising the stages of a process that occurs in a cycle. Notice the key stages of the cycle and the few words to connect these stages together.

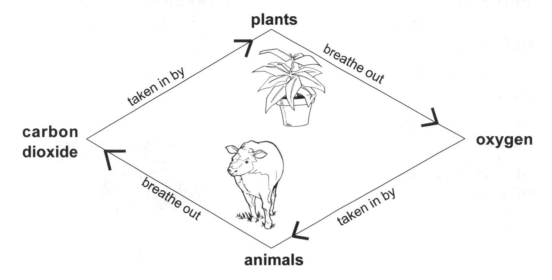

## A CYCLE SUMMARY MAP

- Read the article on moths and butterflies. Choose the term BUTTERFLIES and try to find three other stages that the butterfly goes through in its lifecycle.

- Draw a cyclic map. Write butterflies in position 1. Write in the stage that follows 'butterflies' in position 2. Then write in the stage that follows this stage in position 3 and finally stage 4 in position 4. Write in a few words along each arrow to show what happens for one stage to form the next stage.

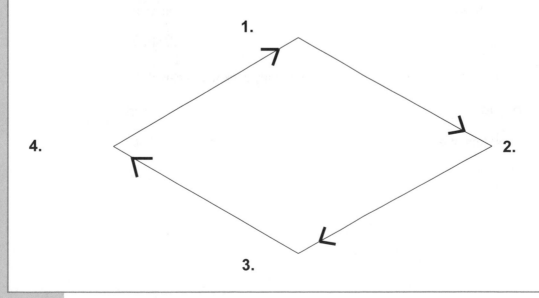

Learn to Think

**1.** Fill in the missing words (?) on the concept maps below.

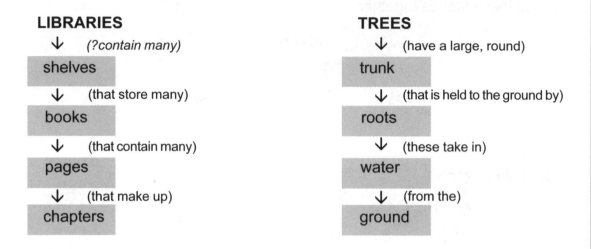

**LIBRARIES**
↓ *(?contain many)*
shelves
↓ (that store many)
books
↓ (that contain many)
pages
↓ (that make up)
chapters

**TREES**
↓ (have a large, round)
trunk
↓ (that is held to the ground by)
roots
↓ (these take in)
water
↓ (from the)
ground

**2.** Complete this summary map.

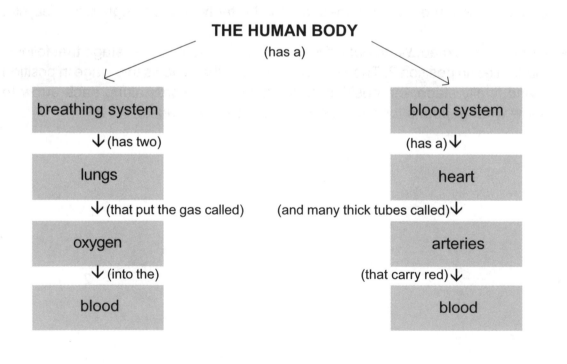

**THE HUMAN BODY**
(has a)

breathing system
↓ (has two)
lungs
↓ (that put the gas called)
oxygen
↓ (into the)
blood

blood system
(has a) ↓
heart
(and many thick tubes called) ↓
arteries
(that carry red) ↓
blood

**3.** Try to make up a summary map for these terms:

sides, quadrilaterals, diagonals, squares, rectangles, angles

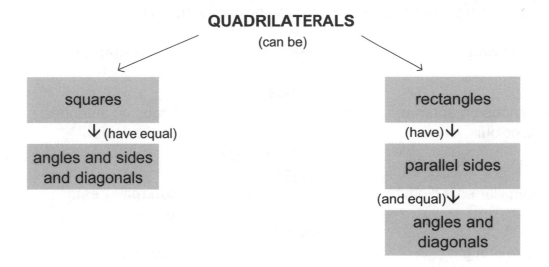

**QUADRILATERALS**
(can be)

squares
↓ (have equal)
angles and sides and diagonals

rectangles
(have) ↓
parallel sides
(and equal) ↓
angles and diagonals

**4.** Look at the picture summary map for comparing TWO THINGS. It is used to summarise and clarify things that are different, and things that are the same, about two things.

| Cats only | Both | Dogs only |
|---|---|---|
| climb trees<br>meow<br>have long fur | have blood<br>four legs<br>house pets | bark<br>have pups<br>like bones |

**5.** Fill in the summary picture map below with some features of bicycles and cars.

| Cars only | Both | Bicycles only |
|---|---|---|
| motor<br>carburettor<br>wind screen<br>gear box<br>dash board<br>registration | lights<br>brakes<br>wheels<br>axles<br>speedos | handle bars<br>small seat<br>chain gears<br>pedals<br>spokes |

**6a).** Read the article about moths and butterflies. Underline any features of them that are interesting to remember. Now write these facts in the correct column of this summary picture map to summarise and clarify the facts.

| Moths only | Both | Butterflies |
|---|---|---|
| no knobs on antennae<br>dull colour | antennae | knobs on antennae<br>very coloured |
|  | scales on wings<br>lay eggs |  |
| caterpillar eats clothes |  | caterpillar eats<br>leaves |
|  | sip nectar |  |
| active at night |  | active in day |

**b)** Draw a cyclic map. Write butterflies in position 1. Write in the stage that follows 'butterflies' in position 2. Then write in the stage that follows this stage in position 3 and finally stage 4 in position 4. Write in a few words along each arrow to show what happens for one stage to form the next stage.

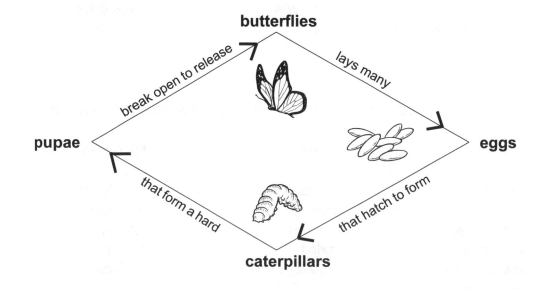

# Analysing Relationships

- Putting together concepts is basic to thinking (Lessons 1-9). Pulling them apart (**analysis**) is just as vital. When faced with raw data or information, we have to break it down (**analyse**) it.
- The questions in this exercise are often found in intelligence tests.
- Good thinkers are quick to analyse the relationship between smaller things and the larger thing that they are part of.

## Example 1

A | bird | is to | feathers | as a | fish | is to |       ?
   **A**           **B**               **C**          **D**

In order to find **D** we have to first find out, or analyse, how **A** and **B** are related. How are feathers related to a bird? Answer: feathers **cover the body of a bird**. So for **D** to have the same relationship with C we have to find **D**, or what **covers the body** of **C** (a fish).

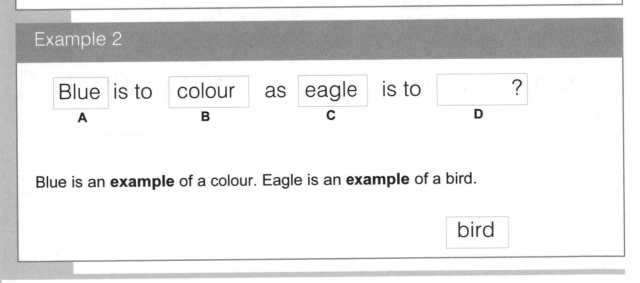

scales

## Example 2

Blue | is to | colour | as | eagle | is to |       ?
  **A**          **B**             **C**         **D**

Blue is an **example** of a colour. Eagle is an **example** of a bird.

bird

- How is **A** related to **B** in each of the following?
- **C** must form this same relationship with **D**.
- When you figure out **D,** write it in on the given line.

| A | is to | B | as | C | is to | D |
|---|---|---|---|---|---|---|
| **stomach** | is to | **food** | as | **lungs** | are to | |
| **triangle** | is to | **three** | as | **square** | is to | |
| **circle** | is to | **sphere** | as | **square** | is to | |
| **artist** | is to | **studio** | as | **judge** | is to | |
| **Sun** | is to | **star** | as | **Saturn** | is to | |
| **oak** | is to | **deciduous** | as | **pine** | is to | |
| **artery** | is to | **blood** | as | **nerve** | is to | |
| **president** | is to | **nation** | as | **mayor** | is to | |
| **retina** | is to | **eye** | as | **ventricle** | is to | |
| **heat** | is to | **energy** | as | **push** | is to | |
| **sing** | is to | **sang** | as | **ride** | is to | |
| **went** | is to | **verb** | as | **dog** | is to | |

## Useful questions to ask myself when ANALYSING RELATIONSHIPS

- 
-

# Lesson Ten

| A | is to | B | as | C | is to | D |
|---|---|---|---|---|---|---|
| **stomach** | is to | **food** | as | **lungs** | is to | **air** |
| (uses/absorbs food) | | | | (use air) | | |
| **triangle** | is to | **three** | as | **square** | is to | **four** |
| (has three sides) | | | | (has four sides) | | |
| **circle** | is to | **sphere** | as | **square** | is to | **cube** |
| (is a flat/2D sphere) | | | | (is a flat/2D cube) | | |
| **artist** | is to | **studio** | as | **judge** | is to | **court** |
| (works in a studio) | | | | (works in a court) | | |
| **Sun** | is to | **star** | as | **Saturn** | is to | **planet** |
| (example of a star) | | | | (example of a planet) | | |
| **oak** | is to | **deciduous** | as | **pine** | is to | **evergreen** |
| **artery** | is to | **blood** | as | **nerve** | is to | **electric signal** |
| **president** | is to | **nation** | as | **mayor** | is to | **city** |
| **retina** | is to | **eye** | as | **ventricle** | is to | **heart** |
| **heat** | is to | **energy** | as | **push** | is to | **force** |
| **sing** | is to | **sang** | as | **ride** | is to | **rode** |
| **went** | is to | **verb** | as | **dog** | is to | **noun** |

## Useful questions to ask when ANALYSING RELATIONSHIPS

- How is the second thing related to the first thing, eg size, colour, use, material, part, shape, example of..?
- What is related to C, or the third thing, in this same way?

Learn to Think

# Analysing Patterns in Sequences

- Here we are going to look at some letter and number sequences.
- You have to write in the last member of each sequence.
- Look carefully at the first three members of each sequence.
- Analyse how the second member changes from the first.
- Now how does the third change from the second?
- Make this same change to the third in order to find the fourth member.

## Examples

| 2 | 6 | 10 | ? |
|---|---|----|---|

The second member of the sequence (6) is the first (2) plus 4.
The third member (10) is the second (6) plus 4.
The fourth member should be the third (10) plus 4 which is 14.

| ABC | ABD | ABE | ? |
|-----|-----|-----|---|

The second member …the last letter increases by one from C to D.
The third member …the last letter increases by one from D to E.
The fourth member should be ABF …AB the same, but last letter goes from E to F.

# Lesson Eleven

Write in the missing member of these sequences. When asked by the teacher, talk aloud about the thoughts you had in finding the missing member to the class.

| | | | | |
|---|---|---|---|---|
| 1. | AA | BB | CC | ...... |
| 2. | AC | CC | EC | ...... |
| 3. | BYB | CYC | ...... | EYE |
| 4. | AAAW | ...... | AAAY | AAAZ |
| 5. | OOXX | ...... | QQXX | RRXX |
| 6. | ZZAA | YYAA | ...... | WWAA |
| 7. | AC | ...... | EC | GC |
| 8. | CAH | CBH | CCH | ..... |
| 9. | ...... | BFGB | CFGC | DFGD |
| 10. | 4 | 9 | 14 | 19 | ...... |

| | | | | | | | |
|---|---|---|---|---|---|---|---|
| 11. | 3 | 4 | 6 | 7 | 9 | 10 | ...... |
| 12. | 2 | 7 | 11 | 14 | ...... | | |
| 13. | 24 | 20 | 18 | 14 | ...... | 8 | |
| 14. | 2 | 4 | 8 | 16 | 32 | ...... | |
| 15. | 3 | 5 | 9 | 15 | ...... | | |

Student worksheet

Draw in the missing information in each sequence.

**16.**

**17.**

**18.**

What is missing in the sequence?

**19.**

**20.**

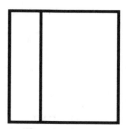 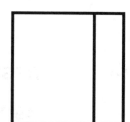 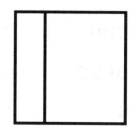  

**21.**

# Lesson Eleven

| | | | | | |
|-----|------|------|------|------|------|
| 1. | AA | BB | CC | DD | |
| 2. | AC | CC | EC | GC | |
| 3. | BYB | CYC | DYD | EYE | |
| 4. | AAAW | AAAX | AAAY | AAAZ | |
| 5. | OOXX | PPXX | QQXX | RRXX | |
| 6. | ZZ | YY | XX | WW | |
| 7. | AC | CC | EC | GC | |
| 8. | CAH | CBH | CCH | CDH | |
| 9. | AFGA | BFGB | CFGC | DFGD | |
| 10. | 4 | 9 | 14 | 19 | 24 |

| | | | | | | | |
|-----|----|----|----|----|----|----|----|
| 11. | 3 | 4 | 6 | 7 | 9 | 10 | 12 |
| 12. | 2 | 7 | 11 | 14 | 16 | | |
| 13. | 24 | 20 | 18 | 14 | 12 | 8 | |
| 14. | 2 | 4 | 8 | 16 | 32 | 64 | |
| 15. | 3 | 5 | 9 | 15 | 23 | | |

16.

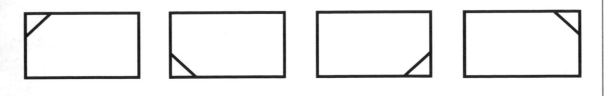

Learn to Think

## Possible answers

**17.**

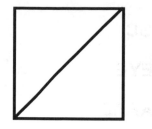 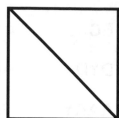 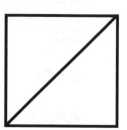 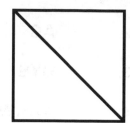

**18.**

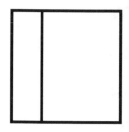 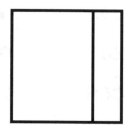 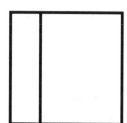 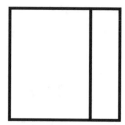

**19.**

**20.**

**21.**

# Distinguishing Facts from Opinions

- When you read the newspaper or magazine, do you believe that every sentence is a fact?
- If you don't, how do you know which sentences are **facts** and which ones are **opinions**?
- This lesson helps you to learn some useful questions that critical thinkers use to identify facts from opinions.
- As you decide which of the following statements are facts and which ones are opinions, try to write down any questions you ask yourself when making each decision.
- Below is a useful list of questions to ask next time you want to distinguish facts from opinions in something you read.

1. Does this sentence contain words such as **could**, **may**, **might**, **possibly**, **predict**, and **should**? (opinions)
2. Could this statement be **proven experimentally** or **with evidence**? If yes – facts. If no – opinion.
3. Is this statement by a **reputable authority**? (fact)
4. Have the things in this statement actually happened or are they happening now? (facts)
5. Does this statement relate to the **feelings** of someone? (opinion)
6. Does this statement contain words like **is**, **has**, **was**, **does**? (fact)

## Examples

| | |
|---|---|
| The Prime Minister of the UK is a man. | **fact** |
| The Prime Minister of the UK should be a man. | **opinion** |

## Student worksheet

Some sentences in newspapers or magazines are facts (F) and some are opinions (O). The sentences here are a mix of both kinds. Think about each sentence here and write in **F**, or **O** after each sentence.

1.      The sun is larger than the moon.

2.      Computers might become as small as molecules one day.

3.      The President of the USA in the year 2020 will be a man.

4.      The sun is more important to us than the moon.

5.      There will be a massive earthquake in China next year.

6.      Dogs make better pets than cats.

7.      Insects have six legs.

8.      We shouldn't produce electricity with nuclear reactors.

9.      We can produce electricity with nuclear reactors.

10.      Men make better pilots than women.

11.      People will live on the moon one day.

12.      It is safer to fly than drive on the roads.

13.      Science is more difficult than History.

14.      Everyone should have a computer.

Now write down some silent questions you asked yourself that allowed you to decide whether something was a fact or whether it was an opinion. Share them with the group and make a list of good questions that will help you to distinguish facts from opinions in future.

A statement is a fact if it:
1.
2.
3.
4.
5.

## Possible answers

**1.** The sun is larger than the moon.                          **fact**

**2.** Computers might become as small as molecules one day.      **opinion**

**3.** The President of the USA in the year 2020 will be a man.   **opinion**

**4.** The sun is more important to us than the moon.            **opinion**

**5.** There will be a massive earthquake in China next year.    **opinion**

**6.** Dogs make better pets than cats.                          **opinion**

**7.** Insects have six legs.                                    **fact**

**8.** We shouldn't produce electricity with nuclear reactors.   **opinion**

**9.** We can produce electricity with nuclear reactors.         **fact**

**10.** Men make better pilots than women.                       **opinion**

**11.** People will live on the moon one day.                    **opinion**

**12.** It is safer to fly than drive on the roads.              **fact**

**13.** Science is more difficult than History.                  **opinion**

**14.** Everyone should have a computer.                         **opinion**

# Distinguishing Definite from Indefinite Conclusions

- Many people jump to conclusions when they see or read things.
- We say they 'read between the lines'.
- They are making inferences, or uncertain conclusions.
- They make up their own conclusions without having definite evidence to support their conclusion.
- People who design advertisements 'suck people in' by making headlines that people draw the wrong conclusions about.
- Here are some examples to try. Don't you jump to conclusions.

## Example

A girl sees a dog panting with its tongue hanging out. She could conclude that:

| | | |
|---|---|---|
| **1.** | it is thirsty. | **inference** |
| **2.** | it has been for a fast run. | **inference** |
| **3.** | it is sick. | **inference** |
| **4.** | it has its tongue hanging out. | **definite conclusion as direct observation** |

The only definite conclusion is 4. There is no evidence for the first three conclusions!

**1.** What can you definitely be **sure** of in this advertisement?  Circle the **two** words that are vague or that can be interpreted in different ways.

*EVERYTHING WILL BE SOLD AT SAINSBURY'S FOR HALF PRICE ON EASTER FRIDAY.*

**2.** A man saw a boy run quickly from a shop . He knocked  a girl down and did not stop to help. Which two of the following can you be **sure** of? Circle them.

a)  the girl was about to go inside the shop.
b)  the boy is late for some reason.
c)  the boy had been in the shop.
d)  the man saw the girl knocked down.

**3.** In the morning Mr Brown found a few of the apples had fallen off his tree onto the ground. Circle the numbers in front of the **two** things here that you think Mr Brown can definitely be **sure** of.

a)  the wind in the night blew the apples off the tree
b)  there are apples on the ground
c)  there will be more apples on the ground tomorrow
d)  the apples had become too ripe
e)  an animal knocked them off the tree
f)  there are still apples on the tree.

**4.** For each of the following events write down **two** conclusions that people might make to explain the event. Choose any one as your conclusion and say what evidence is needed to prove it to be the correct conclusion.

**a)** Your torch doesn't work when you switch it on.

*Conclusion 1:*

*Conclusion 2:*

*I choose conclusion :*
*Evidence needed to prove it:*

**b)** The hardware store is having a closing down sale.

*Conclusion 1:*

*Conclusion 2:*

*I choose conclusion:*
*Evidence needed to prove it:*

**c)** Panda bears are becoming extinct.

*Conclusion 1:*

*Conclusion 2:*

*I choose conclusion:*
*Evidence needed to prove it:*

# Useful questions to ask myself when distinguishing DEFINITE from INDEFINITE conclusions

- 
- 
- 
- 

# Lesson Thirteen

**1.** What can you definitely be **sure** of in this advertisement?  Circle the **two** words that are vague or that can be interpreted in different ways.

(EVERYTHING) WILL BE SOLD AT CITY SAINSBURY'S FOR (HALF PRICE) ON EASTER FRIDAY.

Everything out of fashion or
storm damaged?

Half of what price?
The regular price doubled?

**2.** A man saw a boy run quickly from a shop . He knocked  a girl down and did not stop to help. Which two of the following can you be **sure** of? Circle them.

c)  the boy had been in the shop.        **Directly observable**
d)  the man saw the girl knocked down.    **Directly observable**

**3.** In the morning Mr Brown found a few of the apples had fallen off his tree onto the ground. Circle the numbers in front of the **two** things here that you think Mr Brown can definitely be **sure** of.

b)  there are apples on the ground.        **Directly observable**
f)   there are still apples on the tree.      **Directly observable**

**4.** For each of the following events write down **two** conclusions that people might make to explain the event. Choose any one as your conclusion and say what evidence is needed to prove it to be the correct conclusion.

**a)** Your torch doesn't  work when you switch it on.

*Conclusion 1:*  globe broken      *Conclusion 2:*  batteries flat
*I choose conclusion*: 2          *Evidence needed to prove it:* try new batteries

**b)**  The hardware store is having  a closing down sale.

*Conclusion 1:* owner died      *Conclusion 2:* owner bankrupt
*I choose conclusion:* 1          *Evidence needed to prove it:* ask people in the shop.

**c)**  Panda bears are becoming extinct.

*Conclusion 1:*  Pandas don't reproduce easily
*Conclusion 2:*  they are running out of food
*I choose conclusion:*  2
*Evidence needed to prove it:*  ask zoo managers or check on the internet if food is running low.

Learn to Think

# Challenging the Reliability of a Claim

We often read in the newspaper where someone claims to have seen an unidentified flying object or a strange creature such as Bigfoot or the Loch Ness monster. Your first thought is to ask yourself 'How reliable is this newspaper?' or 'How reliable is the person who wrote this article?' Naturally we want some **proof** or **evidence** before believing them.

A good critical thinker would have some really useful questions that they would want the person making the claim to answer. Here is your chance to think about your questions for judging the reliability of a claim.

## Example

In a newspaper report a man claims to have seen a large, glowing unidentified flying object (UFO) that hovered over the ocean in front of his house. Which **three** of these facts would most help you, or anyone else, **believe** that his report could be true? **Circle** the letter in front of the **three facts** you choose. Why aren't the other observations useful?

a)   The ocean was rough.
b)   He saw it for ten minutes.
c)   There was a new moon.
d)   It was exactly 10 o'clock at night.

e)   He viewed it with his old binoculars.
f )   The friends next door saw it.
g)   The man was 25 years of age.

**Answer:**
- b), e) and f).
- a), d) and g) wouldn't help good or bad viewing.

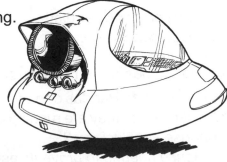

Write **Y** in front of the statements that **help** you to **believe** this claim.
Write **N** in front of the statements that causes you to **doubt** that this claim is true.
Write a **O** in front of the statements that **don't help** you judge this claim.

**Claim:**

1. In 1960 Tor MacLeod claimed that he saw the Loch Ness monster through his binoculars.

2. The large grey mass was about one mile away on the opposite shore.

3. The loch is very deep.

4. The monster had three elephant-like trunks at the front.

5. MacLeod was not accompanied by any of his friends.

6. He had moved to the area to live because he wanted to view the monster before he died.

7. He viewed the monster for about eight minutes.

8. The weather was dull and overcast with the drizzle of rain on the loch.

9. He wore a new overcoat and hat to keep himself warm.

10. MacLeod phoned the newspaper immediately after sighting the monster.

11. The newspaper had just been taken over by a new owner.

1. Write **Y** in front of the statements that **help** you to **believe** this claim.
   Write **N** in front of the statements that causes you to **doubt** that this claim is true.
   Write a **O** in front of the statements that **don't help** you judge this claim .

**Claim:**

1. On November 2, 1957 in Levelland, Texas, a family claimed to have seen a flying saucer.

2. It appeared on the ground, near their car at about 10 o'clock at night.

3. The car was a new one and in very good condition.

4. The family were on their way home after watching an airforce display during the day.

5. They watched the saucer for about five minutes.

6. Several hours later another person saw the saucer in the nearby town.

7. The family said that the engine of their car stopped as the saucer came near.

8. An electrical thunderstorm was in the area at the time of their viewing.

9. The father of the family called the editor of the local newspaper.

10. During the week the paper had run a series of articles on flying saucers.

## Useful questions to ask someone before DECIDING the RELIABILITY of a CLAIM

- 
- 
- 
-

# Lesson Fourteen

1. In 1960 Tor MacLeod claimed that he saw the Loch Ness monster through his binoculars. **O**
2. The large grey mass was about one mile away on the opposite shore. **N**
3. The loch is very deep. **O**
4. The monster had three elephant like trunks at the front. **N**
5. MacLeod was not accompanied by any of his friends. **N**
6. He had moved to the area to live because he wanted to view the monster before he died. **N**
7. He viewed the monster for about eight minutes. **Y**
8. The weather was dull and overcast with the drizzle of rain on the loch. **N**
9. He wore a new overcoat and hat to keep himself warm. **O**
10. MacLeod phoned the newspaper immediately after sighting the monster. **N**
11. The newspaper had just been taken over by a new owner. **O**

1. On November 2, 1957 in Levelland, Texas, a family claimed to have seen a flying saucer. **O**
2. It appeared on the ground, near their car at about 10 o'clock at night. **Y**
3. The car was a new one and in very good condition. **O**
4. The family were on their way home after watching an airforce display during the day. **Y**
5. They watched the saucer for about five minutes. **Y**
6. Several hours later another person saw the saucer in the nearby town. **Y**
7. The family said that the engine of their car stopped as the saucer came near. **Y**
8. An electrical thunderstorm was in the area at the time of their viewing. **N**
9. The father of the family called the editor of the local newspaper. **N**
10. During the week the paper had run a series of articles on flying saucers. **N**

## Useful questions to ask when CHALLENGING the RELIABILITY of a CLAIM

- Did he/she see it first hand and what were the viewing conditions like?
- Did anyone else see it?
- Does he/she have any vested interests in this?
- How close was he/she to the scene and did he/she report this immediately?
- Was he/she of sound mind at the time?
- Is he/she well respected by colleagues?
- Has he/she sought publicity about this issue before?
- How experienced is he/she?
- Was he/she on drugs or alcohol at the time?

Learn to Think

# Distinguishing Relevant from Irrelevant Information

Something is **relevant** if it is 'connected'(to whatever you are thinking about). It may be important in helping you to achieve some purpose or goal you have in mind. For example, what are some relevant factors to consider in choosing a new bike? Choosing a bike is the goal. Is the price relevant? *Yes*. How about the time of day you buy it? *No*.

The more relevant factors or things you can come up with the better will be your decision. First you have to be clear on what your goal is. Then you have to identify what is really important and why.

## Example

Imagine you have lost your dog. Circle the **three** most **important** or **relevant** things here about your dog that you think would help people find it.

a) Where you got the dog from.
c) What the dog eats.
e) The colour of the dog.
g) The height of the dog.

b)  The breed of the dog.
d)  Where the dog sleeps at night.
f)  The sex of the dog.
h)  How fast your dog can run.

**The goal is:** finding your lost dog
Does fact a) help you achieve this goal?
No! It's not important.
The three most important are b), e), f) or g).
Discuss.

# Lesson Fifteen

**1.** You want to apply for an after school job delivering newspapers. The manager asks you to write down some relevant things about yourself that will help you to be considered for the job. Which **three** of the following do you think are most important here?

a)    I am left handed.

b)    I am good at science.

c)    I am a healthy person.

d)    I am 12 years of age.

e)    I am a member of the school basketball team.

f)    I live in the neighbourhood.

g)    I have a new bicycle.

**2.** You want to buy a breakfast cereal that is good for your health. Which **three** things here do you think are most relevant to consider in helping you to make your choice?

a)    The box is made from recycled paper.

b)    Iron Man eats this cereal.

c)    It contains high fibre.

d)    The company is a sponsor of the Olympic Games.

e)    It tastes good.

f)    It doesn't have any preservatives.

g)    It comes in serve size packets.

Learn to Think

**3.** Imagine you have the job of spending a large sum of money to buy some land for a farm. What are **five** very important or relevant properties of the land that you would consider before buying it?

- 
- 
- 
- 
- 

**4.** You have to design a new toy for 3 to 5 year old children to play with. What are **five** very important or relevant features that such a toy should have? Give a reason for each choice.

- 
- 
- 
- 
- 

## Useful questions to ask myself when distinguishing RELEVANT from IRRELEVANT information

- 
- 
-

# Lesson Fifteen

**Question 1:**   c), f) and g)


**Question 2:**   c), e) and f)


**Question 3:**   Quality of soil
Availablity of water
Closeness to roads, transport, etc
Residence or not?
Power or not?

**Question 4:**   Interesting working parts?
Colourful?
Safe?
Educational or useful?
Original?

purpose
properties
goals

## Useful questions to ask when distinguishing RELEVANT from IRRELEVANT factors

• What is the goal or main purpose?

• Which features or properties of the choices definitely help me to achieve this goal?

# Decision Making

Decision making is about using relevant criteria to make a **choice** between some given possibilities. Here is a useful set of strategies:

- Be clear as to what you have to make a decision about or choose between. You might like to state the 'problem' or issue as a question:

  → What will I eat?
  → Who can help me with my homework?
  → How can I make friends?
  → How can I learn to play better basketball?

- Identify the **choices** or alternatives.

  How can I make friends?
  → Pay people to like me.
  → Buy them gifts.
  → Tell them jokes.
  → Be nice to everyone.
  → Smile a lot.

- List the **good** and **bad** things about each choice.
- Identify some relevant **criteria** for comparing the choices. Can it be done? Is it honest? Is it appropriate?
- Compare your choices using these criteria.
- Rate each choice according to the criteria.
  1 = poor, 2 = average, 3 = good in each criteria.
- Make a decision by selecting the best possible choice eg. the choice with the most rating points.

## Useful questions to ask when MAKING A DECISION

- What is the main issue I have to make a decision about?
- What are the choices I can choose between?
- What are the advantages and disadvantages of each choice?
- From these what are some relevant factors to consider in making my decision?
- Can I rate (3,2,1) my choices using these factors?
- Which choice rates most highly overall?

Evaluative Thinking

Learn to Think

# Lesson Sixteen

Decision making involves making a choice between some different alternatives. Before you can do this you need to compare your choices using relevant factors. To find these factors you need to consider some **good** and some **bad things** about each choice.

**1.** Your parents will allow you to buy a family pet. The choice is between a parrot, a dog, a snake, and a rabbit! Write in one good and one bad thing about having each of these animals. Then use these things to identify some **relevant factors** to consider in making a decision about which pet to buy. Share your factors with the class.

| Animal | Good thing | Bad thing |
|--------|-----------|-----------|
| parrot |  |  |
| dog |  |  |
| snake |  |  |
| rabbit |  |  |

Relevant factors to consider in making my decision:

_____

_____

_____

**2.** Imagine you had a choice to become a doctor, a mechanic, an artist, or a teacher. Write down a good thing and a bad thing about having each of these jobs. Then use these things to identify some RELEVANT FACTORS to consider in making a decision about which job you would like. Share your factors with the class.

| Job | Good thing | Bad thing |
|---|---|---|
| doctor | | |
| mechanic | | |
| artist | | |
| teacher | | |

Relevant factors to consider in making my decision:

_____

_____

_____

_____

**3.** Imagine you were shipwrecked on a deserted island. You have to make a camp somewhere on the island. List some factors, or features, of different places on the island you would consider in making your choice. Eg. closeness to river or water supply. Share your factors.

| Factors to consider | Reason why factor important |
|---|---|
| 1.  closeness to water | need to drink every day |
| 2. | |
| 3. | |
| 4. | |

# Lesson Sixteen

**4.** If you had the job of choosing the site for a new airport in a town what are some important or relevant factors to consider about the different places you can choose between?

| Factors to consider | Reason why factor important |
|---|---|
| 1. | |
| 2. | |
| 3. | |
| 4. | |

**5.** Go back to Exercise 1 (p. 65). List your comparing factors on this table. Now give each animal **1** point if it is **poor or bad** in this factor. Give each animal **2** points if it is **average** in this factor. Give it **3** points if it is **good** in a factor. Which animal has the most points? Is this your choice? Why could another animal be an even better choice?

**Animals**

| Factor | Parrot | Dog | Snake | Rabbit |
|---|---|---|---|---|
| | | | | |
| | | | | |
| | | | | |
| | | | | |
| Total points: | | | | |

My choice:

## Useful questions to ask myself when making DECISIONS

- 
-

**1.**

| Animal | Good thing | Bad thing |
|---|---|---|
| parrot | talks, pretty | noisy, messy |
| dog | friendly, can hold/walk | expensive food |
| snake | quiet, not messy | boring |
| rabbit | quiet, eats scraps | messy |

**Relevant factors to consider in making my decision:** noise level, mess made, food costs, interest level.

**2.**

| Job | Good thing | Bad thing |
|---|---|---|
| doctor | big wage | long hours, stress |
| mechanic | outside | messy, boring |
| artist | clean, interesting | poor money |
| teacher | interesting, holidays | stress |

**Relevant factors to consider in making my decision:** salary, stress level, interest level, outside freedom, mess level.

**3.**

| Factors to consider | Reason why factor important |
|---|---|
| 1. closeness to water | need to drink every day |
| 2. shelter from rain | keep dry |
| 3. near food/reef | need to eat/catch fish |
| 4. visible point for help | need to signal boats/planes |

**4.**

| Factors to consider | Reason why factor important |
|---|---|
| 1. closeness to city | cost of bussing |
| 2. closeness to ocean | safety if crash |
| 3. away from homes | don't disturb morning |
| 4. cost of land | expense of project |

**5.**

| Factor | Animals | | | |
|---|---|---|---|---|
| | Parrot | Dog | Snake | Rabbit |
| 1. low food costs | 1 | 1 | 3 | 2 |
| 2. low mess made | 1 | 2 | 3 | 2 |
| 3. high interest level | 2 | 3 | 1 | 1 |
| 4. low noise level | 1 | 2 | 3 | 3 |
| Total points: | 5 | 8 | 10 | 8 |

My choice: a snake! Maybe some factors are more important than others. How can I make them more important?

# Considering Other Points of View

- In an argument most people see only *their* point of view.
- They don't want to hear the other person say why he or she believes something else.
- A good critical thinker is more tolerant and is prepared to at least listen to **the other point of view**.
- Fights and even wars start because people don't want to listen to the other point of view.
- If they did, they might hear some new facts and they might understand the feelings of other people.

## Example

People in some poor countries of the world are cutting down large numbers of their forests. Write down **two** reasons to support or agree with their removal of forests. Write down **two** reasons to disagree with their actions.

**Points for:**
1. It brings in millions of dollars to the country to help the education and health of citizens.
2. It helps employ thousands of people in the forest industry.

**Points against:**
1. It causes erosion of the soil which can be washed away with rains.
2. It means more carbon dioxide gas in the atmosphere because trees feed on it. This in turn means the temperature of the air increases.

# Lesson Seventeen

**1.** Some people think that farmers should not spray insecticides onto their crops. Farmers think they should.

Write in **two** reasons why farmers shouldn't and **two** reasons why farmers should spray insecticides on their crops.

**Why they shouldn't:**

- 
- 

**Why they should:**

- 
- 

**2.** Some people think that it is wrong for some countries to kill whales. The people who kill the whales believe they should be allowed to kill them.

Write in **two** reasons why people shouldn't kill whales and **two** reasons why people from some countries should be able to kill whales.

**Why shouldn't kill whales:**

- 
- 

**Why should kill whales:**

- 
- 

## Useful questions to ask MYSELF when considering OTHER POINTS OF VIEW

- 
-

**1.** Some people think that farmers should not spray insecticides onto their crops. Farmers think they should.

Write in **two** reasons why farmers shouldn't and **two** reasons why farmers should spray insecticides on their crops.

**Why they shouldn't:**

- Insecticides poison insects then birds.
- Insecticides on skins of crop: eaten by humans.

**Why they should:**

- Insects could ruin crops.
- Farmers wouldn't grow crops if couldn't kill insects.

**2.** Some people think that it is wrong for some countries to kill whales. The people who kill the whales believe they should be allowed to kill them.

Write in **two** reasons why people shouldn't kill whales and **two** reasons why people from some countries should be able to kill whales.

**Why we shouldn't kill whales:**

- Some whales will become extinct.
- Food whales feed on will increase dangerously.

**Why we should kill whales:**

- Some cultures depend on whale meat in diet.
- Whaling employs many people.

## Useful questions to ask when considering other POINTS OF VIEW

- Am I unfairly biased in my belief about this issue?
- Do I know all the facts on both sides of this issue?
- Why does this person have an opposite point of view?
- Why do I have my point of view?

# Asking Better Questions

- Most people find it difficult to ask someone else questions about something they are talking about.
- Most pupils wait to answer questions rather than ask their own.
- Yet **the more questions you can ask yourself** about something you read or hear, the more likely you will understand what it is about.
- When you ask a question, you attend more carefully and you make connections with things you already know.
- **The better your questions the better your thinking**, especially your critical thinking.

The seven basic question words:

**How?** eg. How does TV influence public opinion?
**Why?** eg. Why do people tell lies?
**What?** eg. What are the main causes of the disease?
**Where?** eg. Where can I find information?
**When?** eg. When is the best time to make a plan?
**Which?** eg. Which is the best choice to make?
**Who?** eg. Who can I trust?

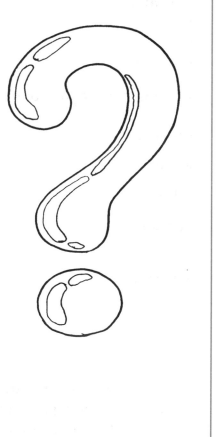

## Part 1
The Why? or How? Question Maker

**1.** Write in 1 to 5 words along each line to make a sentence.

Flowers _____ seeds.

Flowers _____ leaves.

Flowers _____ thorns.

Flowers _____ colours.

Now ask WHY? or HOW? after each sentence to make some questions. See how you can make interesting questions about any thing! Maybe the teacher will blackboard 5 to 10 of the best questions from the group for the class to answer.

Answers:
- 
- 
- 

**2.** Repeat this again for whales.

Whales _____ mammals.

Whales _____ migrate.

Whales _____ fish.

Whales _____ noises.

Answers:
- 
- 
- 

**3.** Repeat this for a few more topics that the group would like to make questions about. Write the topic at the start of the line. Write some important words about the topic at the end of the lines. Now to see how you can do this for making up questions about anything you read.

# Lesson Eighteen

Student worksheet

**4.** Read this passage about the topic of INSECTS. Pick out **four** key words that are especially about insects. Now make up **four** sentences starting with the word *Insects* and ending with words you have chosen.

### Insects

*Insects are small, six legged animals. Flies, moths, and ants are just a few kinds of insects. Insects have two antennae on their heads that they use to detect smells. Their bodies have three segments or parts that contain holes that they breathe through. Insects have two sets of wings. Some insects are helpful to humans and some are harmful. Most insects lay hundreds of eggs.*

Insects _____

Insects _____

Insects _____

Insects _____

Answer the best questions about insects from the group.

## Part 2
Two word question starters

Student worksheet

This is another way of making your own questions.

1.  Choose the first word for your question from Row A.
2.  Choose your second word from row B.

| A. | What | Where | When | Which | Who | Why | How |
|---|---|---|---|---|---|---|---|
| B. | is/are/do | did/was | would/could/can | might | | | |

3.  Now make your sentence starting with these words.

Learn to Think

Evaluative Thinking

75

Example topic: CLOUDS

| | |
|---|---|
| **What are** | clouds made of? |
| **Why are** | clouds of different shapes? |
| **Who would** | be interested in clouds? |
| **Where might** | you not find any clouds? |
| **How are** | clouds made? |

Using the words in Row A and Row B, you should be able to make 30 or more interesting and different questions about clouds. Imagine the number of new connections in your brain about clouds!

**4.** As a group select a topic eg. flowers, flies, birds, trees, sports.

- Each person try to make up **four** questions about the chosen topic.
- Use different question starters from rows A and B.
- Share your questions with the group to get a large number of group questions
- Now see how many the group can answer.
- Repeat this task but choose another topic.

# Lesson Eighteen

## Part 1
### The Why? or How? Question Maker

**1.** Flowers.

- Flowers have many seeds. Why? Flowers need many seeds because not many grow when they hit the ground.

- Flowers are surroundeed by leaves. Why? Flowers need leaves that take in carbon dioxide as food for the flower.

- Flowers sometimes grow thorns. Why? Thorns protect the flowers from being eaten by wild animals.

- Flowers come in many colours. Why? The colours of a flower attract many bees that take the pollen of the flower to fertilise other flowers.

**2.** Whales.

- Whales are examples of mammals. Why? Because they have warm blood, a backbone, and give birth to live babies.

- Whales swim a long way to migrate. Why? Because they swim to warm waters to give birth to their young.

- Whales are not fish. Why? Because whales have lungs and not gills.

- Whales often make loud noises. Why? To attract other whales to swim and mate together.

**3.** Words from Insects reading: **antennae, wings, harmful, eggs**

- Insects have two long antennae. Why? Insects use antennae to sense nearby objects and food.

- Insects have two sets of wings. Why? Insects need spare wings in case they damage some.

- Insects are sometimes harmful. How? Some insects eat crops, eat clothing, eat timber.

- Insects lay thousands of eggs. Why? Insects need many eggs because predators eat them for food.

# Creative Consequences

- Creative thinking involves escaping, or breaking away, from the usual ways of doing, making, using, or thinking about things.
- One way of doing this is to fantasise or dream of way out ideas about a subject.
- Young people are experts at thinking in this way in their play before they come to school.
- In this exercise, you can think about the consequences of some unlikely or impossible event occurring.
- You will notice that other people will have *different* ideas to yours. But like all questions that involve creative thinking, there is no one correct answer.

## Examples

If there were no more TREES in the world then...there would be less oxygen in the air...and this would mean many people would die in the big cities.

If we ran out of ELECTRICITY... then it would mean the end of computers, television and all but face to face communication.

If I decided not to get ANGRY again, no matter what...then I might make more friends, and I might be happier.

# Lesson Nineteen

Complete the following by placing words in the blanks.

**1.** If there were no more birds in the world then _____

_____

and this would mean _____

**2.** If the Earth no longer had a moon then _____

_____

and this would mean _____

**3.** If there was no longer any oil deposits on Earth then _____

_____

and this would mean _____

**4.** If there was no longer any whales on Earth then _____

_____

and this would mean that _____

Make up some more 'if _____ then' statements for the class to complete in a funny and imaginative way.

**1.** If there were no more birds in the world then there would be more insects and this would mean more leaves of plants eaten.

**2.** If the Earth no longer had a moon then no more tides and this would mean the bottom of ocean not stirred for fish to feed.

**3.** If there was no longer any oil deposits on Earth then no petrol could be made and this would mean that cars would become useless.

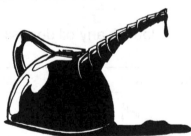

**4.** If there was no longer any whales on Earth then no longer whale hunters and this would mean that some countries would have to find other meat to eat and other chemicals that come from whale oil.

# Reverse Creative Thinking

- Creative thinkers often try an idea that is just the opposite of what most people would try.
- They try reverse thinking. This really loosens up those fixed patterns you have stored in your brain.
- Your brain remembers what you **can** photograph, or what you **can** see. But it hurts when it has to come up with things you **can't** photograph or **can't** see. This lesson will help you to escape the usual patterns stored in the brain.

## Example

**Question:** List three places where you *can't* find air.

**Answers:** In space, in a light bulb, in a vacuum, inside a rock.

**1.** List **three** things that you **could not** photograph with your camera.

- 
- 
- 

**2.** List **three** ways of opening a book **without** holding it with your hands.

- 
- 
- 

**3.** What are **three** reasons why a person is seen reading a newspaper with it turned **upside down**?

- 
- 
- 

**4.** What are **three** ways in which a car and a tree are the **same**?

- 
- 
- 

**5.** List **three** things that you **would not** find in the U.K.

- 
- 
- 

Creative Thinking

# Lesson Twenty

**1.** Three things you could not photograph: A feeling, a sound, the universe, infinity, the core of the Earth, people long dead.

**2.** Three ways you could open a book without using your hands: Open it with your mouth, hold string placed between the pages, use a vacuum cleaner, get someone else to open it, use some sticks or a knife and fork.

**3.** Three reasons why a person was seen reading a newspaper with it turned upside down: They are hiding from someone, they are shading themselves, they are blind, only the outside page is upside down.

**4.** Three ways in which a car and tree are the same: They both take in and give off gases, they provide shade, they are of many different types, shapes, and colours, they have many parts,

**5.** Three things you would not find in the UK: Dinosaurs, pyramids, Disneyland, giant redwood trees.

# Analyzing the Creativity of Designs

- Creative people are sensitive to the creativity about them.
- That is, they notice the design of things created by humans or by nature.
- Everything about us ( dogs, trees, pencils, ourselves, cars) has a design that fits a particular function.
- The more you carefully observe things and ask yourself *why* it has its particular shape, colour, size, shape, material, parts, and hardness, the more sensitive to creativity you will be.
- You are asking the same questions that passed through the mind of the first person to make the things about us.

## Examples

**Question:**
Why are bottles made of glass rather than some other material? There has to be a reason why the first person to make a bottle chose the material glass.

**Possible answers:**
Glass is easy to clean, glass is clear so we can see what is inside easily, glass melts easily so is easy to blow into shape of a bottle.

**Question:**
Why is a tennis ball round?

**Possible answers:**
So that it rolls easily.

**Question:**
Why is a tennis ball soft, with a hollow centre?

**Possible answers:**
So that it is light, and can be hit easily (and without danger to the players).

# Lesson Twenty-one

Everything about you has a design that fits a special purpose. Even things in nature. If the design is not the best then nature or humans change it so that the design really fits its special purpose. You look at things each day but do you ever question why something has the creative design that it has? Here is your chance.

**1.** Why do pencils usually have six sides rather than three or ten?

**2.** Why does a tree have 1000s of leaves rather than four or five?

**3.** Why are newspaper pages so big compared with the pages of a book?

**4.** Why are drinking cups made of clay rather than steel?

**5.** Why do dogs and cats have four legs rather than two or six?

**6.** Why is the colour red used to indicate danger or to be alert ?

**7.** Why are tyres made of rubber?

Learn to Think

**8.** Why do forks have four prongs rather than two or ten?

**9.** Why are coins usually round?

**10.** Why are stamps usually rectangular?

**11.** Why are road signs usually white writing on a green background or yellow writing on black background?

**12.** Why do fish have scales?

**14.** Why are coins often made of copper?

# Useful questions to ask myself when ANALYSING the CREATIVE DESIGNS of NATURE and HUMAN BEINGS

- 

-

# Lesson Twenty-one

**1.** Why do pencils usually have six sides rather than three or ten?

Easier to hold, make, store in boxes, don't roll.

**2.** Why does a tree have 1000s of leaves rather than four or five?

Leaves are the mouth and nose of tree to take in food or carbon dioxide. Trees can't move around Earth to gather food like animals. They need many mouths (pores in leaves), and hence leaves, to gather food.

**3.** Why are newspaper pages so big compared with the pages of a book?

To keep papers thin, so don't need to bind papers, cheaper to make and print, easier to get rid of.

**4.** Why are drinking cups made of clay rather than steel?

Clay doesn't get too hot to hold, easier to make clay cups by machine, don't lose heat of drink too quickly.

**5.** Why do dogs and cats have **four** legs rather than **two** or **six**?

Run faster, 2 legs needed for holding bones/meat,  6 legs hard to coordinate.

**6.** Why is the colour red used to indicate danger or to be alert ?
Red colour is most irritable colour to the eye and makes it pay attention quickly.

**7.** Why are tyres made of rubber?

Flexible so soft ride for driver, easy to make and repair, wear slowly.

**8.** Why do forks have **four** prongs rather than **two** or **ten**?

Four prongs make a scoop to lift up food, ten would be hard to clean between prongs and two prongs wouldn't form a scoop.

**9.** Why are coins usually round?

Easy to make, no sharp edges to hold, easy to store, easy to put in machines.

**10.** Why are stamps usually rectangular?

Easy to print, easy to make a sheet of stamps, east to tear off sheet,

**11.** Why are road signs usually white writing on a green background or yellow writing on black background?

Green on white and yellow on black are the most contrasting colour combinations to the eye and are most easily noticed.

**12.** Why do fish have scales?

Scales keep fish warm, easy to flow through water, hard to catch hold of.

**13.** Why are coins often made of copper?

Copper doesn't rust, copper forms alloy that is strong and it doesn't bend.

**Useful Question:** Why does this thing have certain **SCUMPS?**

# Creativity from Random Objects

This strategy is good for creative problem solving, creative writing, and creative product design. It enables you to escape the usual way of thinking about these tasks by making unexpected links via an unrelated object.

## Examples

1. Think of an object that has nothing to do with the task in hand.
2. Write down five or so features of this object.
3. Try to use one of these features at a time to make a creative link with the problem, the writing, or product to improve. Not all features of the random input will be useful.

**Task 1:**

To solve the problem of a dirty school yard.

**Random object:** a pencil
**Features:** pointed, coloured, hexagonal shape, wooden, 'lead', breaks easily.

**Solutions:**

- Divide yard into *coloured* zones. Each class to be responsible for cleanliness of a particular coloured zone.

- Students found littering yard have to wear a ***coloured, hexagonal*** badge for a day.

# Lesson Twenty-two

**Task 2:**

To describe a person in a story.

**Random object:** a pencil
**Features:** pointed, coloured, hexagonal shape, wooden, lead, breaks easily.

**Description:**

Mr Policeman has a ***pointed*** nose and a ***hexagonal*** shaped face that turns a variety of ***colours*** when he is cross. He walks as if he has ***wooden*** legs.

**Task 3**

To improve the design of drinking glasses.

**Random object:** a pencil
**Features:** pointed, coloured, hexagonal shape, wooden, lead, breaks easily.

**Improvements:**

Make the glasses with ***hexagonal*** or six sides. Make each glass in the set a different ***colour*** to help people identify their glass, place them in a ***wooden*** holder for easy movement from the kitchen.

**Task 1:**

Write a brief description of a football player.

**Random object:** a car tyre
**Features:** rubbery, thick, wears out, round, noisy, rough, (add more).

**Your description:** (include the words from above)

Jack the football player _____

_____

_____

_____

**Task 2:**

Improve the design of a packet of breakfast cereal to make it sell better.

**Random object:** a flower
**Features of object:** Different colours, scented, seeds, petals, different shapes, (add more).

Suggested creative changes to design _____

_____

_____

_____

**Task 3:**

How to reduce the number of cars on city roads.

**Random object:** a newspaper
**Features of object:** pages, stories, numbers, index, crosswords, pictures, (add more)

Solutions to problem: _____

_____

_____

_____

# Visual Creativity

Our brains mainly remember usual or common shapes (patterns) and what these shapes represent. We can learn to think flexibly about ideas and patterns after seeing how people think flexibly by escaping their fixed patterns.

In the following five minute exercises, you will get a score.

A score of:   **0-3** categories of ideas suggests low flexibility (creativity)
**4-7** categories suggests average flexibility
 **8+** categories suggests high flexibity

## Example

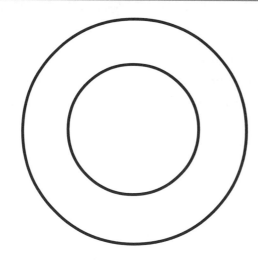

**Possibilities:**

doughnut
tyre
bullseye
person's eye
ring
clock
door handle
hat, looking down from above
compass
cassette tape
sticky tape
button
saucer/plate
CD
etc

Learn to Think

**1.** In five minutes, write down as many different things this line drawing could represent. Then we will change papers and your partner will mark as many acceptable answers that you have. These must be agreed upon by most of the class.

**2.** In five minutes write down as many different things this line drawing could represent. Then we will change papers and your partner will mark as many acceptable answers that you have. These must be agreed upon by most of the class.

# Creative Thinking about Uses

- This is an exercise to help you think more flexibly about uses of something.
- The brain remembers that the usual use for a brick is to build a wall, a house, a building, and so on which are all in the category of a **vertical structure**.
- The creative or flexible thinker can break away from usual uses and think of other categories of uses.

## Example

Write down all the possible uses for a table.

Write down all the properties (or attributes) of a table, and then list other things that also use that property.

| Properties | Possible uses |
| --- | --- |
| • flat, smooth surface<br>• stable structure<br>• straight edges<br>• moveable | • draw on, drive toy cars on<br>• podium or stage, and stacking to make a column<br>• tear paper, measure things<br>• stand on edge and use as a display surface, stand upside down and use as a 'room'. |

**1.** In five minutes write down all of the usual and unusual uses you can think of for a brick. The uses should be quite different from each other.

Features or properties of a brick: _____
_____
_____
_____
_____

Possible uses for a brick: _____
_____
_____
_____
_____

**2.** In five minutes write down all of the usual and unusual uses you can think of for a newspaper. The uses should be quite different from each other.

Features of a newspaper: _____
_____
_____
_____
_____

Possible uses for a newspaper: _____
_____
_____
_____
_____

# Lesson Twenty-four

## Student worksheet

**3.** In five minutes write down all of the usual and unusual uses you can think of for a piece of string. The uses should be quite different from each other.

Features of a piece of string: ______________________________

______________________________

______________________________

______________________________

______________________________

Possible uses for a piece of string: ______________________________

______________________________

______________________________

______________________________

______________________________

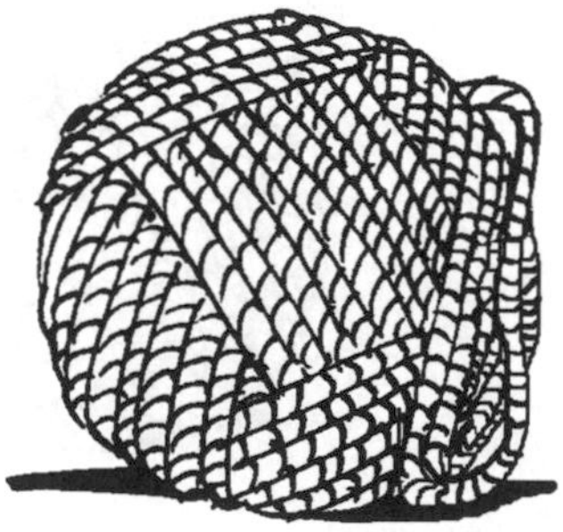

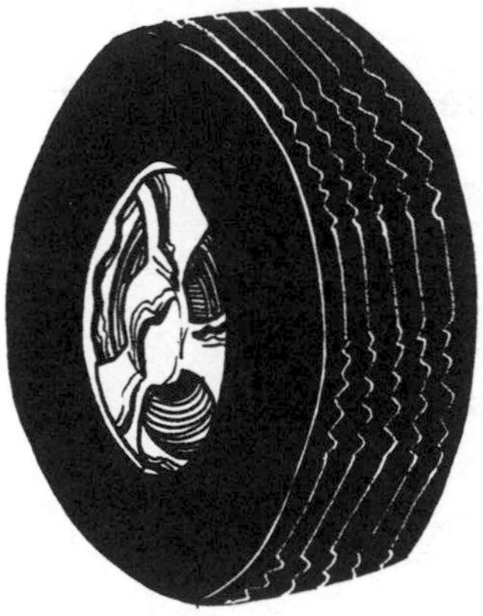

**4.** In five minutes write down all of the usual and unusual uses you can think of for a car tyre. The uses should be quite different from each other:

Features of a car tyre: ______________________________

______________________________

______________________________

______________________________

______________________________

Possible uses for a car tyre: ______________________________

______________________________

______________________________

______________________________

______________________________

**1.** In 5 minutes write down all of the possible uses for a brick.

Uses...**rough** – an abrasive, **heavy** – weapon, hammer, door stop, paper weight, to lift, **holed** – pencil holder, home for insects, **straight edges** – a ruler, a border, to build vertical walls, to build paths, **bulky** – to stand or sit on, a ramp in gutter, a car tyre wedge, support, **coloured** – to make marks.

**2.** In 5 minutes write down all of the possible uses for a newspaper.

Uses...**porous** – clean windows, blot ink or water, **large area** – cover windows, cover floors, wrap food in, cover books  **light** – make kites, light fires, **flexible** – wrap glass in, stuff shoes.

**3.** In 5 minutes write down all the possible uses of a piece of string.

**thin** – shoe laces, fishing line, clothes line, book mark.

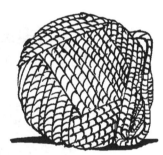

**4.** In 5 minutes write down all the possible uses for a car tyre.

**round** – hoop to roll, border for plants, seat for a swing, **elastic** – for boats against wharf, to make roads, for racing cars to crash into, **bulky** – tyre reefs for fish to live in.

0-3 low flexibility of thought, 4-7 average flexibility of thought, 8+ good flexibility of thought.